Project AIR FORCE

A FRAM FOR MODERNIZATION WITHIN THE UNITED STATES AIR FORCE

T0097943

Glenn A. Kent
David A. Ochmanek

Prepared for the
UNITED STATES AIR FORCE

RAND

The research reported here was sponsored by the United States Air Force under Contract F49642-01-C-0003. Further information may be obtained from the Strategic Planning Division, Directorate of Plans, Hq USAF.

Library of Congress Cataloging-in-Publication Data

Kent, Glenn A., 1915-
  A framework for modernization within the United States Air Force /
Glenn A. Kent, David A. Ochmanek.
    p. cm.
    "MR-1706."
    ISBN 0-8330-3427-8 (pbk.)
    1. United States. Air Force—Reorganization. 2. Military planning—United
states. I. Ochmanek, David A. II. Title.

UG633.K45423 2003
358.4'00973—dc21

2003010854

RAND is a nonprofit institution that helps improve policy and decisionmaking through research and analysis. RAND® is a registered trademark. RAND's publications do not necessarily reflect the opinions or policies of its research sponsors.

Published 2003 by RAND
1700 Main Street, P.O. Box 2138, Santa Monica, CA 90407-2138
1200 South Hayes Street, Arlington, VA 22202-5050
201 North Craig Street, Suite 202, Pittsburgh, PA 15213-1516
RAND URL: http://www.rand.org/
To order RAND documents or to obtain additional information,
contact Distribution Services: Telephone: (310) 451-7002;
Fax: (310) 451-6915; Email: order@rand.org

Since assuming the position of Chief of Staff, Headquarters, United States Air Force in 2001, General John Jumper has sought to invigorate the process of modernizing the operational capabilities provided by the Air Force. Central to his approach has been a focus on *concepts of operation* (CONOPs) to achieve operational capabilities, as opposed to hardware or programs, as the centerpiece of thinking about and describing those capabilities. General Jumper has elected to pursue an approach involving "task forces" (teams) and the concepts they would employ to achieve important operational objectives in future conflicts. He has designated officers to serve as "champions" for promoting new concepts that provide key types of operational capabilities and for monitoring the status of these within the Air Force's programming and budgeting process.

This report offers a broad conceptual framework for promoting innovation and modernization within the Air Force that is consistent with General Jumper's emphasis on operational concepts and capabilities. It aims to help the Air Staff implement General Jumper's approach in several ways: First, it offers a clearly defined set of terms relevant to the consideration of military capabilities and concepts at several levels of operation. Second, it identifies (generically) the principal actors within the Air Force who are responsible for guiding and promoting innovation. Third, it lays out a process governing the interactions among these principal actors, encompassing activities that range from strategic planning to providing the operational capabilities needed by warfighting units. Finally, this report offers the leadership of the Air Force a listing of operational capabilities, derived from the defense strategy and from joint-service employment concepts, that could be used to organize the efforts of the "champions" designated by General Jumper.

This report should be of interest to practitioners and students of force planning and modernization. The project documented here was conducted within the Strategy and Doctrine Program of RAND's Project AIR FORCE. Comments are welcome and may be addressed to the authors or to the Program Director, Dr. Edward Harshberger.

PROJECT AIR FORCE

Project AIR FORCE (PAF), a division of RAND, is the Air Force's federally funded research and development center for studies and analyses. PAF provides the Air Force with independent analyses of policy alternatives affecting the development, employment, combat readiness, and support of current and future aerospace forces. Research is performed in four programs: Aerospace Force Development; Manpower, Personnel, and Training; Resource Management; and Strategy and Doctrine.

Additional information about PAF is available on our Web site at http://www.rand.org/paf.

CONTENTS

FIGURES

Like its sister services, the Air Force is charged, by Title 10 of the U.S. Code, with providing combatant commanders with capabilities that fulfill, to the maximum extent practicable, their operational requirements. In a highly dynamic security environment, when threats faced by the United States are changing rapidly and the types and nature of operations conducted by its forces are changing as well, it is especially important that the services effectively promote innovation and modernization of their operational capabilities. Instituting a straightforward, coherent, and well-defined process for modernizing can help the leaders of the Air Force ensure that relevant capabilities are developed and fielded in a timely manner.

Functionally speaking, seven principal actors are involved in the modernization process within a service. They are:

- **The Definer,** whose chief role is to frame a finite set of high-priority operational challenges (or requirements) that the Air Force will strive to meet. Meeting these challenges involves developing new concepts for fielding new or significantly improved capabilities. (See pages 11–14.)

- **The Conceivers,** who formulate, define, and, when appropriate, demonstrate new *concepts of execution* (CONEXs), where a CONEX is an end-to-end concept for accomplishing a particular operational task. (See pages 14–15.)

- **The Proponents,** who define new *concepts of employment* (CONEMPs), where a CONEMP is a concept for achieving a particular operational objective. Each Proponent is responsible for monitoring and assessing the Air Force's capabilities to achieve a related set of operational objectives. The Proponents also seek to ensure that adequate resources are allocated within the Air Force to sustain and advance "their" set of operational capabilities. They also serve as advocates for resources to authorities outside of the Air Force (for example, in the Office of the Secretary of Defense and in Congress). (See pages 27–30.)

- **The Independent Evaluators,** who advise the Secretary of the Air Force and the Chief of Staff on the merit of any proposed new concepts. (See pages 31–33.)

- **The Programmers,** who estimate the cost of proposed concepts and suggest ways for balancing resources across all of the activities that the Air Force carries out. (See pages 16–17.)

- **The Providers,** who provide *capabilities* (not forces) to combatant commanders by implementing new CONEXs and new CONEMPs. The acquisition of new platforms, weapons, and support systems falls under this rubric. (See pages 18–19.)

- **The Secretary of the Air Force and the Chief of Staff,** who preside over the entire process outlined above and render decisions at key points. Their responsibilities include the issuance of an approved list of operational challenges, the choice of whether to pursue a concept proposed by the Proponents, and how best to advocate that concept to gain the resources needed to implement the concept.

The system for spurring and managing innovation within the Air Force can be essentially fully established by defining the responsibilities of each of the aforementioned actors and the relationships among them. The framework we describe is depicted in Figure S.1.

Seven Proponents, each a senior officer on the Air Staff, could cover the operational capabilities of greatest saliency to the Air Force. Their areas of responsibility could be defined as follows:

RAND*MR1706-S.1*

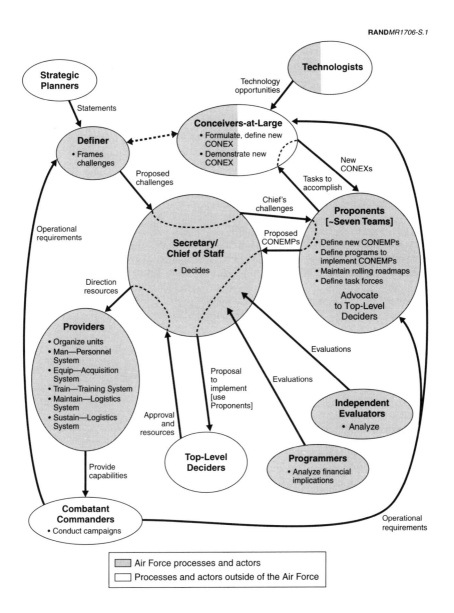

Figure S.1—The Master Framework for Modernizing: A Service Perspective

- **Team 1: Gain freedom to operate.** This goal encompasses efforts to establish access in theaters of operations, to gain air superiority and space superiority over the enemy, and to sustain high-tempo operations at bases in the theater despite countervailing actions by the enemy.

- **Team 2: Provide control of the operation of forces.**

- **Team 3: Provide strategic air mobility.**

- **Team 4: Fight and gain the effects desired in conflicts.**

- **Team 5: Protect the homeland.**

- **Team 6: Conduct global strikes.**

- **Team 7: Conduct other operations.** This objective includes maintaining global awareness, providing a stabilizing presence in key regions, and providing humanitarian relief.

Chapter One

INTRODUCTION

BACKGROUND

Modernizing the operational capabilities provided by the Air Force is a journey, not a one-time event. Modernizing yields "transformation" and a revolution in military affairs (RMA) when the capabilities of the force are dramatically superior to (or different from) those that have come before. But discussions of whether the Air Force is (or is not) transforming are of little purpose. The Air Force modernizes (as it has in the past) as opportunities appear. The Air Force has been on the journey, seizing opportunities to meet new challenges, for many years, and it shows.

The words "modernizing operational capabilities" were chosen with some care. We could have used the words "modernizing forces"— but that would suggest that the "forces" (types of units) remain the same and that we are simply modernizing existing types of platforms or units. More often than not, quantum jumps in operational capabilities have been achieved in the past when new types of forces were conceived. For example, dramatically new capabilities emerged when vehicles that operated in new mediums (such as in the air and in space) were introduced.

There is another reason to talk in terms of capabilities. The Air Force provides capabilities to combatant commanders and achieves these capabilities according to a concept of employment (CONEMP) defined by the Air Force. If a service thinks of itself as simply "providing forces" to combatant commanders, it diminishes its role in the development of operational art within its medium.

PROMOTING INNOVATION: THE 5000 MODEL

To hasten the journey of modernizing, we need an institutional framework that promotes innovation and timely progress. This is not an idle point. Many officials in the Department of Defense (DoD) preach transformation and innovation but at the same time tolerate an approach for governing modernization, embodied in the "5000 model" and the "requirements generation system," that does anything but.[1] Taken at face value, according to the 5000 model, any service wishing to enter into an activity called "concept and technology development" (or in a later paragraph "concept exploration") must pass Milestone A. Milestone A is the first formal step in the "Defense Acquisition Management Framework." According to current DoD directives, at Milestone A the Milestone Decision Authority (MDA)—a person designated by the Under Secretary of Defense for Acquisition, Technology, and Logistics (USD/AT&L)—can, among other things, permit one to "enter concept and technology development."[2] The concept and technology development phase, in turn, is defined as having "two major efforts: concept exploration and technology development." Taken literally, this directive would compel a service to go through a lengthy bureaucratic process to gain permission to explore new operational concepts. This effort to systematize and centralize control over thinking about innovation runs counter to experience and to common sense, both of which suggest that good ideas most often bubble up from people engaged in trying to solve concrete problems.

It is not only the acquisition system that lays claim to authority over creative endeavors within DoD; the "requirements generation sys-

---

[1]The 5000 model refers to Department of Defense Directive No. 5000.1, *The Defense Acquisition System*, USD(AT&L), October 23, 2000, which specifies the formal process by which services are to conduct the development, testing, and management of new systems. The requirements generation process refers to efforts presided over by the Joint Requirements Oversight Council (JROC) intended to develop sets of "validated requirements"—essentially performance specifications for new systems.

[2]Deputy Secretary of Defense memorandum, *Defense Acquisition*, October 30, 2002, Attachment 2, p. 4. (See http://dod5000.dau.mil.)

tem" asserts itself as well. To pass Milestone A and enter into concept exploration, one must first provide an "initial capabilities document" (ICD). The controlling document states that the ICD contains statements "of broad, time-phased operational goals and describe requisite capabilities."[3] So far, so good. Such a statement would be very much like the operational challenges that are a centerpiece of our proposed framework.

An ICD, in our view, should be a statement about the need for a certain type of operational capability written in broad operational terms; for example, "USAF forces need better means to protect forward bases against attacks by enemy ballistic missiles." But if this is what is today meant by an ICD, why do we need a very complicated process to develop, "validate," and "approve" such a statement? Again, the controlling document states that an "analysis of capability solution sets" must *precede* the development of the ICD. That analysis must encompass "potential concepts across the DoD components, international systems from Allies, and cooperative opportunities; and an assessment of the critical technologies associated with these concepts...."[4] Requiring all of this work on potential solutions prior to stating a broad operational goal seems to be putting the cart before the horse.

The ICD, like the Mission Needs Statement (MNS) before it, has, in practice, become a definition of the characteristics of the system that is intended to provide some operational capability. By entwining burdensome acquisition-related certifications with the process of identifying needs and exploring new operational concepts, DoD has inhibited innovation by compelling would-be innovators to engage in a mystifying array of "filling squares" prior to engaging in exploration of new concepts.

PROMOTING INNOVATION: A BETTER MODEL

This report presents a model that adheres to the goal of promoting timely innovation in modernizing operational capabilities. It seeks to reemphasize the distinctions between concept development,

---

[3]Ibid.
[4]Ibid.

which plays the central role in determining *what* systems to pursue, and acquisition, which is properly focused on *how* to develop and procure such systems. The 5000 model, which governs the acquisition of systems, should not aspire to control thinking and experimentation essential to the development of new capabilities and concepts.

The perspective taken here is that of a service that takes seriously its obligation to develop and field forces with enhanced and relevant operational capabilities, and to do so on a timely basis.[5] The model we advocate calls on the services to take the initiative in developing and proposing new operational capabilities. The Joint Requirements Oversight Council (JROC) and the Office of Program Analysis and Evaluation (PA&E) principally evaluate those proposed concepts, making recommendations to the DoD leadership about which ones merit implementation. The goal is to minimize the constraints and strictures placed upon those charged with generating innovation and to create a more-level playing field on which new concepts can compete for resources.

Our model has the following general characteristics:

- The model is "actor oriented," as distinct from "document oriented." It defines the roles of the various actors in fostering and promoting modernization.

- The model's actors address matters that are focused at the operational and tactical levels, as distinct from a focus at the campaign level (a level higher).

- The model ignores any supposed requirement to ask, "May I?" from some higher authority before engaging in the art and science of exploring new concepts.

- The model promotes enduring activities associated with the exploration and development of new concepts at three levels: (1) new concepts of systems and platforms, (2) new concepts for accomplishing military tasks, and (3) new concepts for achieving operational objectives.

---

[5]For more on the importance of distinguishing between concept development and system development, see Glenn A. Kent and David E. Thaler, *A New Concept for Streamlining Up-Front Planning*, RAND, MR-271-AF, 1993.

- By deriving operational challenges, objectives, and tasks from an examination of potential joint-service campaigns, the model promotes a joint perspective.

- The model is straightforward and adheres to a rigorous lexicon. This is not a trivial virtue, considering the proliferation of undisciplined vernacular and confusing slogans at large within the U.S. defense community today.

The utility of a simple and coherent model (even though it may not be officially adopted) is especially evident when there is no obvious model to follow; or, if one exists, it lacks logic and coherence. Trying to change flawed models within a large bureaucracy is generally a lost cause. Rather, one should devise and apply one's own model to set a steady course and to guide one through the maze. At the same time, it is permissible (and is often necessary) to engage in the square-filling required by officialdom, knowing that these actions are largely digressions.

Finally, the model presented here builds on the approach promoted by General John Jumper, Chief of Staff of the Air Force—an approach that places operational capabilities at the heart of the process of modernizing and that designates "champions" for developing new concepts to provide various types of operational capabilities.

THE REPORT

The central purpose of this report is to describe a model, or conceptual framework, for modernization within the Air Force. The remainder of the report is organized as follows:

- In Chapter Two, we define key terms used in the model.

- In Chapter Three, we present and explain the overall model and the roles of the principal actors within it.

- In Chapter Four, we describe the challenges—as set forth by the actor called the "Definer."

- In Chapter Five, we focus on the actors called "Proponents."

- In Chapter Six, we take a closer look at the activities of the "Independent Evaluators."

- In Chapter Seven, we offer some thoughts about organizational matters relating to the overall framework.
- Finally, in Chapter Eight, we provide some remarks about documents.

Chapter Two

THE LEXICON

Before addressing the overall model, it is useful to define the primary elements of the lexicon.

FOUR LEVELS OF ACTORS

First, we offer a lexicon relevant to military operations in a theater war. There are four levels of actors in this hierarchy:

- The national level—the President, Secretary of Defense, and the Chairman of the Joint Chiefs of Staff (CJCS)

- The campaign level—the overall commander responsible for planning and overseeing a military campaign, usually a four-star regional or functional combatant commander

- The operational level—the subordinate commanders (for example, the joint forces air component commander) and the operational controllers

- The tactical level—the combatants and the tactical controllers.

CONCEPTS OF OPERATIONS

A concept of operations (CONOP) defines the means for achieving a stated objective. As with the actors, we can define the objectives to be achieved by military operations at four levels: national, campaign, operational, and tactical. Thus the term CONOP could, in principle, apply to any level. To avoid confusion we adopt the following lexicon:

- At the national level: The President, the Secretary of Defense, and the CJCS define the wars to wage, the *campaigns* to conduct, and the overall effects to be attained by these campaigns.

- At the campaign level: The combatant commander defines the *campaign operations plan* (or campaign strategy) to achieve the desired effects in a stated campaign. More specifically, the combatant commander defines the operational objectives to be achieved over time.

- At the operational level: The subordinate commanders define the *"concept of employment"* (CONEMP) to achieve each of the stated operational objectives or to conduct a major operation within the campaign. More specifically, the subordinate commander defines the military tasks to be accomplished over time.

- At the tactical level: The combatants define *concepts of execution* (CONEXs) to accomplish each of the stated military tasks.

In the above construction, a CONEX for a military task is defined to include all of the major assets that must be brought to bear to accomplish that task successfully, from the launch of sorties to their recovery. For example, in the case of engaging and killing elusive targets, the CONEX includes the finders, controllers, and the shooters. The CONEX prescribes

- How the "finders" detect, identify, and locate the target,

- How the "tactical controller" assigns a particular shooter to engage a particular target, and

- How the "shooter" then engages the target, the shooter being defined by both the platform and weapon.

As such, a CONEX defines the means by which these assets—finders, controllers, and shooters—are to be integrated "horizontally" in the accomplishment of each task.

Again, we use the term CONEX to refer to a means of accomplishing some stated task. A CONEMP is a way of achieving some stated operational objective. There is a connection between the two. Operational objectives generally encompass multiple tasks. For example, one operational objective is to delay, damage, and destroy an advancing ground force. The subordinate commander may seek to achieve that objective by accomplishing several tasks: interdicting lines of communication; destroying stocks of fuel and other supplies used by the advancing force; and attacking the forces themselves. Hence, if one improves the CONEX for accomplishing a particular task, one may also change the CONEMP for achieving the operational objective, altering the way forces are employed and the weight of effort applied by U.S. forces against certain tasks over time.

LACING THEM TOGETHER

Now to lace the levels, actors, and concepts together (from the bottom up):

- Combatants accomplish a portfolio of military tasks (according to the CONEX for each stated task). By doing so, they enable a subordinate commander (in the presence of a CONEMP) to achieve some stated operational objective (or to conduct some stated major operation within a campaign).

- Subordinate commanders achieve a portfolio of operational objectives (according to the CONEMP for each objective). By doing so, they enable the overall combatant commander (in the presence of a campaign strategy) to attain the effects desired in conducting the campaign.

EFFECTS-BASED OPERATIONS

The idea of talking about "effects" is not new. What may be new is the idea of focusing on effects at the campaign level—above the tactical and operational. But the idea of effects holds at all levels:

- Protecting and advancing the security interests of the United States is a statement about effects at the national level.

- Compelling and coercing a particular rogue leader to accede to U.S. terms is a statement of effects at the campaign level.

- Halting an invasion over a period of time is a statement of effects at the operational level.

- Destroying an array of enemy combat units in an engagement is a statement of effects at the tactical (or engagement) level.

We make two observations from the above: First, to hold an informed discussion about "effects," one must first specify the level at which one is dealing—national, campaign, operational, or tactical. Second, statements about effects are really no different from statements about objectives. An example at the operational level is: (a) the operational objective is to halt the invasion short of a specified point; (b) the effect the commander desires to attain is a halt of the enemy advance short of this objective. At the campaign level: (a) the objective is to compel/coerce an enemy leader to accede to U.S. demands; (b) the effect the combatant commander seeks to attain is a surrender by the rogue leader.

ON OPERATIONAL REQUIREMENTS

Our lexicon incorporates the term "operational requirements." We use it to refer to statements of challenges at the operational level. For example, it is reasonable to state that there is an operational requirement today to field improved capabilities to thwart attacks by theater ballistic missiles on forward deployed forces and bases. Likewise, there is an operational requirement to develop better means for locating and identifying suspected terrorist groups or individuals in complex terrain.

Too often, the term "operational requirement" is applied to statements such as "there is an operational requirement for this system" or, worse, "there is a requirement that a particular system attain this level of performance." We specifically reject these constructions and hold that the term "operational requirement" should refer to the need for an operational *capability*. The term should not be used to refer to a specific system or type of system. The logic is simple: The term "requirement" is a statement about need, not a statement about solution. Moreover, attaching the term "requirement" to a system or its characteristics can lead one to treat the system, which is often only one of several possible means to an end, as somehow sacrosanct, blinding one to the possibility of other approaches.

Chapter Three

THE OVERALL MODEL FOR MODERNIZING

We propose that the Air Force leadership adopt the overall model shown in Figure 1 as its process for governing efforts to modernize the operational capabilities it provides to combatant commanders. Our depiction of the model adheres to three very simple principles:

- A circle (or an ellipse) depicts one of the principal actors involved.

- Labels or arrows that go from one actor to another show the inputs and outputs attendant to each of the actors.

- Within each circle there is a terse statement as to the actor's functions or processes; that is, how the actor provides each output.

THE STRATEGIC PLANNERS AND THE DEFINERS

The process starts in the upper left-hand corner of Figure 1 with the strategic planners. These planners reside in the Office of the Secretary of Defense (OSD) and in the Joint Staff. They reside, as well, in the National Security Council (NSC) staff and in various think tanks. They issue a series of statements regarding the future operating environment, the possible missions of the U.S. armed forces, and the types of capabilities that they believe will be most relevant to future military operations.

These planners' statements, being framed at a high level of generality, are not always directly useful in defining the types of

11

RAND*MR1706-1*

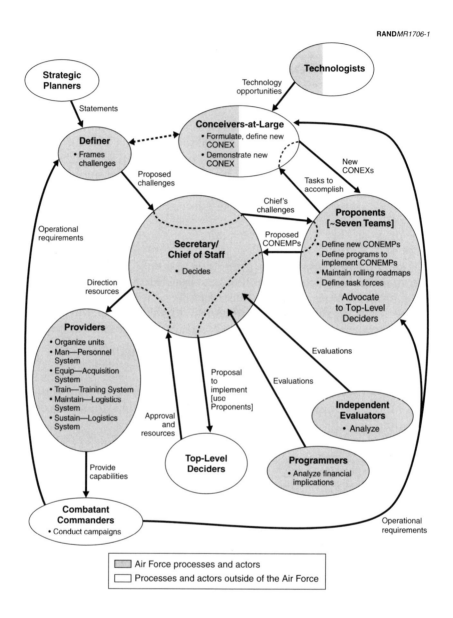

Figure 1—The Master Framework for Modernizing: A Service Perspective

operational capabilities the Air Force intends to provide. For that reason, our model also features a "Definer" within the Air Force who defines what these statements mean in terms of the types of operational capabilities to be provided by the Air Force.

For example, translating such terms as "rapid decisive operations," "dominant maneuver," and "precision strike" into statements of challenges on which the Air Force will focus is not a straightforward proposition. The "Definer" is thus shown as a principal actor. Surveying the changing security environment, participating in the development of defense strategy, and helping to identify looming shortfalls in the capabilities of joint forces are a full-time job for a creative major general.

The output of the Definer, then, is a set of challenges—statements that, when approved by the Secretary and the Chief of Staff of the service, task the corporate Air Force to develop operational capabilities appropriate to meeting each challenge. These challenges can be considered operational requirements, in accordance with the Air Force's principal responsibility under Title 10 to provide capabilities that fulfill, to the maximum extent practicable, the operational requirements of the combatant commands.[1] This being the case, it is important that the challenges be derived from an examination of joint-service campaigns and that they be phrased in terms of operational objectives assigned to joint forces. The Definer, thereby, should identify not "Air Force" challenges, but rather a set of challenges faced by joint forces, which the capabilities of U.S. Air Force (USAF) forces can help to address. For this reason, the figure shows the combatant commanders communicating their operational requirements to the Definer, the Proponents, and the Conceivers.

The Definer's statement of challenges sets the overall direction for all that follows. Decisions about developing new capabilities cast a long shadow ahead. Suppose a Conceiver develops a new concept for fulfilling a particular challenge. If a new major system (platform) is required to implement the concept, seven to ten years or more may pass before the new capability is a reality; and the concept may en-

---

[1]United States Code, Title 10, Sec. 8013.

dure for another 20 years or more. Thus, we are casting a shadow 30 years or so hence.

For these reasons, the set of challenges developed by the Definer is sent to the Secretary and the Chief of Staff for their review, adjustment, and, finally, approval. In Chapter Four we suggest a set of these operational challenges.

THE PROPONENTS

The next principal actors in this process are the "Proponents." Their primary function is to develop, in response to the operational challenges, new concepts of employment—new concepts that will enable USAF forces, operating in conjunction with the forces of other services, to achieve important operational objectives even in the face of enemy resistance.

The primary input to each team of Proponents is one (or more) of the Chief's challenges. Each team is challenged to promote new CONEXs and define new CONEMPs so that the Air Force can provide improved capabilities to fulfill this operational requirement—now and, especially, in the future.

Chapter Five amplifies the roles of the Proponents.

THE CONCEIVERS-AT-LARGE (AT THE TASK LEVEL)

Another input to the Proponents, generally in the form of new CONEXs, stems from the Conceivers-at-Large. The Conceivers, in turn, have two primary inputs: (1) a knowledge of existing and emerging technologies, and (2) statements from the Proponents as to the military tasks that merit the greatest emphasis.[2] With these two inputs, the Conceivers "connect the dots." They define concepts for accomplishing stated military tasks and, when appropriate, conduct field tests to demonstrate promising new concepts.

---

[2]The Conceivers are also cognizant of the operational challenges put forth by the Definers, as is shown by the dotted line connecting the two in Figure 1.

The output of the Conceivers-at-Large is an evolving portfolio of CONEXs from which each Proponent can pick and choose. Not infrequently, a particular CONEX may be a player in more than one CONEMP; thus the name "Conceivers-at-Large." The Conceivers operate across the board—across the portfolio of operational challenges.[3]

BACK TO THE PROPONENTS

In the presence of new CONEXs generated by the Conceivers, the Proponents formulate, define, and demonstrate new concepts (CONEMPs) for achieving stated operational objectives. Episodically, the Proponents then propose to the Secretary and the Chief that they approve the proposed concept and that they seek authority and resources to implement it. There is a role for people in the "joint world" to participate in the development of new CONEMPs. People at Joint Forces Command, on the Joint Staff, at the headquarters of combatant commands, and elsewhere may devise creative ways to translate the pieces (CONEXs and systems) developed by the military services into CONEMPs (at the operational level) that meet the needs of combatant commanders. Generally, however, operators and technologists in the services will be best positioned to formulate new CONEXs (at the tactical or task level).

THE SECRETARY AND THE CHIEF OF STAFF

The Secretary and the Chief of Staff now decide whether to approve the concept as proposed (or amended). If they elect to proceed, they propose to the Top-Level Deciders (the Secretary of Defense and his principal advisors) that the concept be implemented and that resources be allocated to develop the hardware, facilities, and other assets required to make the concept a reality.

---

[3]For more on the role and process of concept development, including a description of the work of an ad hoc concept development group, see J. L. Birkler et al., *Gaining New Military Capability: An Experiment in Concept Development*, RAND, MR-912-OSD, 1998.

THE INDEPENDENT EVALUATORS

The Secretary and the Chief of Staff, in their deliberations regarding what to propose to the Top-Level Deciders, rely heavily on the Independent Evaluators. The Proponents, of course, conduct their own evaluations, which focus mainly on a single operational objective. Specifically, each Proponent seeks to determine which among several candidate CONEMPs will best achieve the stated operational capability for which he or she is responsible.

The Independent Evaluators also address the issue at this level, but with a focus at a level higher as well. More specifically, they address how resources should be allocated among the full range of CONEMPs being considered and proposed by the Proponents. The Independent Evaluators, then, strive to shed light on whether to implement the proposed CONEMP in the face of competing demands for resources. This leads to determining the best marginal return of investments among competing CONEMPs and their associated operational objectives in order to attain desired effects at the campaign level. This daunting analytical problem is addressed in Chapter Six.

FINANCIAL MANAGERS AND PROGRAMMERS

Over time, the Proponents will advocate the implementation of a number of CONEMPS. Before deciding yea or nay, the Secretary and the Chief of Staff must hear from the Independent Evaluators regarding the value of each concept in terms of operational capabilities. The financial manager and the programmer will determine the financial implications after estimating the full costs of adapting a new CONEMP and the resources required on a year-by-year basis. They determine if the concept would fit into the overall Air Force budget— again, year-by-year. The Programmer is obliged to inform the leadership if the Proponent has significantly underestimated the cost to implement the concept.

The financial manager and programmer should be proactive in attaining resources. They will probably tell the Secretary and the Chief of Staff that implementing the concept now will cause a bow-wave that exceeds an expected level of resources in some of the out-years of the USAF's program. However, they should also act as entrepreneurs and attempt to be creative in financing the proposed concept. They can, for example, suggest possible areas for reductions of other items within the Air Force program. They can also suggest approaches for gaining resources beyond the Air Force's projected total obligational authority (TOA).

THE TOP-LEVEL DECIDERS

Once a proposed CONEMP has made its way through each of the actors described above, the Air Force is ready to approach the Top-Level Deciders—the Secretary of Defense and his principal advisors, chiefly the Under Secretary for Acquisition, Technology, and Logistics (USD/AT&L). The input to the Top-Level Deciders is a proposal; their output, it is hoped, is approval and allocation. The Top-Level Deciders base their decisions on the same criteria as the Air Force's Secretary and the Chief of Staff, namely:

- Is the CONEMP technically feasible?

- Is the CONEMP operationally viable?

- Is the capability provided by the CONEMP relevant in conducting important military operations?

- Is the CONEMP consistent with policy and other political constraints?

- How well does the CONEMP measure up against competing CONEMPs on the basis of marginal return?

- Is the acquisition program to acquire any system associated with the CONEMP executable?

Based on the answers to these criteria, the Top-Level Deciders decide to implement the CONEMP (or not to implement it). In approaching each decision, the Top-Level Deciders will surely organize actors (players) at their level to advise them. These players include:

- Technologists from the Director, Defense Research and Engineering (DDR&E), who inform the Deciders about technical feasibility

- Combatants from the Joint Chiefs of Staff (JCS) and the combatant commands, who inform the Deciders about operational viability

- Strategists from OSD and the JCS, who determine if the proposed CONEMP is consistent with U.S. policy and if the operational objective the CONEMP seeks to achieve is relevant

- Analysts from PA&E, who inform the Decider about the allocation of resources based on marginal return of the CONEMP compared with allocating resources to various other CONEMPs for different operational objectives

- Cost analysts, who inform the Top-Level Deciders about the projected cost to implement the concept

- Acquisition experts, who attest whether the program to develop and acquire any system to implement the concept is executable.

The above construction is based on the idea that a service can probably be counted on to propose the best CONEMP within the realm of its operations (air, land, sea, or space) to achieve a stated type of operational capability. The expertise is in the service, which has every incentive to propose the best CONEMP. On the other hand, a particular service may not be an unbiased witness regarding whether resources should be allocated to implement the CONEMP it has proposed, as opposed to CONEMPs proposed by other services. Accordingly, independent analyses about the marginal return on investment are quite appropriate.

Once the Top-Level Deciders have rendered their decision to implement a concept, and they inform the Secretary and the Chief of Staff of their decision, the Secretary and the Chief direct the Providers and allocate resources accordingly.

THE PROVIDERS

The input to the Providers is direction to proceed. That is, they are directed to provide the stated operational capability by implementing the proposed CONEMP within a given level of resources and according to a certain schedule. Implementing a new concept involves (or could involve) several functions:

- Organizing units

- Manning the units with trained personnel

- Equipping the units with systems, weapons, and other hardware

- Training the operators in the units

- Maintaining the units in peacetime

- Sustaining the units in combat operations.

Consider, for example, the concept of deploying three satellites, equipped with infrared sensors in geosynchronous orbit, to detect the launch of intercontinental ballistic missiles (ICBMs)—a CONEMP generally known as the Defense Support Program (DSP). Once the Top-Level Deciders decided to implement this concept, the Air Force:

- Organized new units to operate these satellites

- Manned the units with trained personnel through the Air Force personnel system

- Equipped the units with the appropriate systems through the Air Force acquisition system

- Trained the personnel in these units through a formal training system and through on-the-job training (OJT) within the units

- Maintained and sustained the equipment associated with the units through a logistics system.

Thus the Air Force, by implementing the CONEMP and by sustaining operations over the years, provides a certain type of operational capability to various combatant commanders.

As stated earlier, the acquisition system equips units with systems. Because Title 10 prohibits the Secretary of the service from delegating the oversight of system acquisition to the service chief, the Secretary and his staff play the leading role in this important function.

In closing, the Provider's output is operational capabilities that are available to the combatant commands. Or, as stated succinctly in Title 10, the primary responsibility of the Air Force (like the other services) is "to fulfill, to the maximum extent practicable, the operational requirements of the combatant commands."

Chapter Four

THE CHALLENGES DEFINED BY THE DEFINERS

We are mindful of the fact that the Air Force, as a corporate body, does not plan and wage wars, plan and conduct campaigns within a war, or even conduct major operations within a campaign. Air Force personnel engage in these activities, but not in the name of the corporate Air Force. However, the Air Force is responsible for providing operational capabilities that, along with capabilities provided by other services, fulfill, to the maximum extent practicable, the operational requirements (both current and projected) of the combatant commands. Such capabilities should enable the combatant commanders to prevail quickly and decisively (and to gain the effects desired) in campaigns.

Having said this, it still behooves each service to define explicitly and carefully those operational objectives and military tasks on which they intend to focus their efforts. These can be framed as challenges. Defining these challenges is an art form. The Definer must operate in an environment of changing operational requirements and emerging technologies. As we have already observed, the direction the Definer sets today will help to determine how some future combatant commander will conduct a campaign 20 or 30 years later. Because we cannot predict the future with any fidelity, we must assume that this hypothetical future campaign will take place in a region not now specified and for some cause not now known. Under these circumstances, the term "*setting* the direction" seems more appropriate than "*planning* the direction" of the Air Force or the Department of Defense.

Even so, there must be stability in the vectors given to Proponents and Conceivers. If the direction is changed substantially every four years, the system will become unstable. The theory of guidance systems tells us that if the time to respond to a particular signal (direction) is longer than the time between different directions, one is in real trouble. Despite all of the above, we now muster the courage to frame a set of operational challenges relevant to the Air Force. These challenges, originally framed by the Definer, are generally in the context of "objectives to achieve" and "tasks to accomplish." The "objectives to achieve" appear in all capital letters, with the associated tasks (broadly defined) in bullets beneath.[1]

GAIN AND MAINTAIN FREEDOM TO OPERATE

- **Establish Access**

  — Gain access to bases (in a political sense); maintain access to the bases (in an operational sense); protect the bases; deploy forces rapidly to the bases; sustain high tempo operations from the bases.

- **Provide Control of the Operation of Forces**

  — At the tactical level—provide dynamic engagement control of finders, controllers, and shooters in accomplishing military tasks.

  — At the operational level—ensure the right combatants are at the right place at the right time, prepared to accomplish the military tasks set forth.

  — Maintain situational awareness of the battle space.

- **Gain Air Supremacy**

  — Conduct effective operations in the air and from the air, and deny the same to the enemy. This challenge includes such tasks as shooting down enemy aircraft in flight, attacking

---

[1]For background on the "strategies to tasks" approach and for more complete derivations of operational tasks, see David E. Thaler, *Strategies to Tasks: A Framework for Linking Means and Ends*, MR-300-AF, RAND, 1993.

them on the ground, and suppressing or destroying ground-based enemy air defenses, such as surface-to-air missile batteries and associated command-and-control sites.

- **Establish Space Supremacy**

  — Conduct effective operations in space and from space and deny the same to the enemy.

- **Provide Strategic Air Mobility**

  — Airlift joint forces and support assets between and within theaters.

  — Provide aerial refueling to aircraft deploying and conducting operations.

FIGHT AND GAIN THE EFFECTS DESIRED IN CONFLICTS

- **Interdict Enemy Forces,** especially large-scale invasions, whether on land, sea, or air

- **Prepare the Battlefield**

  — Disrupt, damage, and destroy enemy ground units.

  — Counter enemy aircraft, ballistic missiles, and cruise missiles attempting to attack friendly ground forces.

- **Support Friendly Land Force Operations,** especially in the context of evicting enemy forces from disputed areas (including but not limited to close air support)

  — Provide fires to curtail the movement of enemy forces and enable the immediate plan of maneuver of friendly forces.

- **Disrupt Enemy Unit Operations,** especially elusive units in wooded areas, caves, and urban environments and those enemy units about to do harm

  — Locate, identify, and destroy or fix small units of enemy forces.

- **Damage/Destroy the Enemy's Central Infrastructure** (leadership, military, economic)
- **Provide Combat Search and Rescue**

CONDUCT AND SUPPORT ENDURING OPERATIONS

The third grouping centers on capabilities (objectives) generally not part of a major regional campaign.

- **Maintain Global Awareness,** especially about the activities and capabilities of adversary states and terrorist groups
- **Provide Homeland Security,** especially from attacks by terrorists or by states armed with nuclear weapons
  - Deter or prevent attacks if possible and alleviate effects if prevention fails.

- **Conduct Global Strikes**
  - Locate, identify, and destroy military units and terrorist groups associated with nuclear, biological, chemical, and radiological weapons and their means of delivery, as directed by the President and the Secretary of Defense.
  - Locate, identify, and destroy infrastructures associated with nuclear, biological, chemical, and radiological weapons and their means of delivery.

- **Provide a Stabilizing Presence in Key Regions**
  - Provide advice and assistance to friendly governments for suppressing terrorist and insurgent groups.
  - Conduct peace operations.

- **Provide Humanitarian Assistance at Home and Abroad**

ESTABLISHING PRIORITIES

Of course, not all challenges are created equal. Some are inherently more crucial to the success of a particular operation or type of operation than others. Some operational objectives may, for a time at least, be uncontested by the enemy. For example, U.S. military forces in operations during the post–Cold War era have enjoyed essentially uncontested access to space and use of space-based assets. This has allowed the Air Force over the past several years to place a fairly low priority on the development of concepts and associated systems for countering potential threats to space assets. This situation may change and prudence dictates efforts to anticipate such changes.

Numerous tasks are associated with most of the operational objectives listed above. For the "Chief's challenges" to be most useful, some sense of relative priority must be attached to each of them; otherwise, scarce human and material resources may be spread too thin, impeding efforts to develop the most salient new capabilities. To focus resources, the Definer, the Secretary, and the Chief of Staff must render judgments regarding the importance that should be placed on particular types of operations and particular threats that may emerge in the future. This, in turn, will yield a rough ranking among the operational objectives, pointing to those challenges where the greatest emphasis seems called for.

Chapter Five

THE PROPONENTS

We envisage that a Proponent be designated to oversee the efforts by the Air Force for each of the operational challenges set forth above. The Proponent for a particular challenge would formulate and define concepts for meeting the challenge—both CONEMPs and attendant CONEXs. After evaluating various concepts (and, when appropriate, demonstrating promising concepts), the Proponent would recommend to the Secretary and the Chief of Staff that certain concepts be implemented.

Each Proponent is aided in his endeavors by the Conceivers-at-Large, who abide at several places: at Headquarters Air Combat Command (HQ/ACC), at Headquarters Air Force Materiel Command (HQ/AFMC), in the labs, at Defense Advanced Research Projects Agency (DARPA), and elsewhere. At each location, they formulate and define concepts for accomplishing military tasks and reveal these concepts (CONEXs) to the relevant Proponents.

Although the Proponents focus generally on the operational level, they must be quite expert at how to accomplish tasks (at the tactical level). This is so because operational objectives are most often achieved by accomplishing a portfolio of associated military tasks. At the same time, the Proponents must think in terms of campaigns in order to assess the relevance of achieving stated operational objectives.

There are feedback loops between the various Conceivers and the Proponents. The Conceivers "surf the net" of Proponents searching for an application of the CONEX they are promoting. At the same time, the Proponents surf the net of Conceivers, looking for new

CONEXs that can address important shortfalls in the capabilities of fielded and programmed forces.

In our construct, the Proponents generally do not deal with technologists directly; rather, they deal with the Conceivers. The reason is straightforward: Technologists converse in terms of the performance levels of hardware. For example, they deal in such commodities as effective radiated power (ERP), explosive power (in tons), and how to keep time at a level of accuracy of less than a microsecond. On the other hand, Conceivers should think in terms of accomplishing operational tasks. Their focus should be on such matters as disabling radars with directed-energy weapons from stand-off platforms, how to destroy enemy aircraft in shelters, and how to determine position in some reference geoid down to a few meters by listening to signals from several satellites. By the same token, we do not promote the idea that Conceivers directly propose to the Secretary and the Chief of Staff that a particular new CONEX be implemented. The Proponents do this.

The following episode demonstrates why advocacy should be by the Proponents at the level of operational objectives. In the early 1970s, the Air Force was considering three candidate munitions for cratering runways at enemy airfields: Munition A, under development by the Air Force's Armament Division; another munition under development by the labs at Livermore; and a third munition being developed by the French, called Durandal. The Armament Division conducted a cost-effectiveness analysis comparing the three weapons. Perhaps not surprisingly, Munition A was declared the winner, and the Armament Division recommended that the Air Force proceed to develop and procure that weapon.

However, when analyzed at the operational level the answer was "buy none of the above." In terms of operational-level outcomes, there were better uses of the sorties available. The reasons for this were evident: (1) many weapons were required to have high confidence of closing an airfield; (2) there was apt to be considerable attrition to aircraft attempting the mission; and (3) the craters could be filled rather rapidly. In short, while the CONEX developed by the Conceivers at the Armament Division represented an improvement over the capabilities of the forces existing at that time, the degree of improvement was not sufficient to warrant the investment of resources needed to realize it.

This example illustrates that the trade-space at the task level is constrained to the best means of accomplishing a stated task. By contrast, the trade-space at the operational level is expanded and involves comparisons among different CONEXs to determine the best mix and level of effort among various tasks. For this reason, before proposing that resources be allocated to implement a CONEX to accomplish a stated task, the Proponents should examine whether accomplishing the stated task in this manner (and at this level of effectiveness) represents the best allocation of resources (in this case sorties) in the first place.

The Proponents will also be counted on to assist the Secretary and the Chief of Staff in their advocacy of selected concepts to Top-Level Deciders. Here the trade-space is much larger. The Top-Level Deciders (outside of the Air Force) consider not only a particular operational objective, but look simultaneously across all operational objectives. This means that prior to deciding to advocate a new concept, the Secretary and the Chief of Staff must be prepared to argue that improving any particular operational capability according to a specific CONEMP represents a wise investment when compared with investing resources in other CONEMPs to achieve other operational objectives. (Analyses at this level are discussed in the next chapter.) It also implies that Proponents should have a clear understanding of how USAF capabilities operate in conjunction with the capabilities provided by other services.

Finally, each Proponent is responsible for assessing the ability of joint forces to achieve the operational objectives to which he or she has been assigned. These assessments should be set in three time periods: today, at the end of the Program Objective Memorandum (POM) period (five to six years hence), and as projected (about 15 years into the future). Each Proponent is also responsible for monitoring the status of key programs that contribute to the capabilities most relevant to the Proponent's objectives. For example, the Proponent for "Freedom to Operate" monitors the status of such programs as the F-22, the airborne laser, hardening of bases, and other programs to provide the capability to fend off threats to friendly bases. This Proponent monitors as well the status of political arrangements to facilitate access to bases. The assessment by each Proponent of capabilities and associated programs is reflected in a "rolling roadmap." Once generated, these rolling roadmaps can be valuable sources of information on where the Air Force spends its resources and how it is planning to evolve in meeting the challenges put forth by the Chief of Staff.

Chapter Six

THE INDEPENDENT EVALUATORS AND THE ART OF ADVOCACY

In our construct, the Independent Evaluators work for the Secretary and the Chief of Staff, informing them at three levels of analysis:

- Has a particular Proponent made the right trades within a particular type of operational capability? Here the trade-space is *within* an operational objective.

- Does implementing the particular CONEMP (and attendant CONEXs) represent best marginal return when compared to implementing new concepts to provide other types of operational capabilities on which the Air Force is focusing? Here the trade-space is *among* the portfolio of operational objectives and capabilities on which the Air Force is focusing.

- How does the proposed CONEMP stack up when compared to CONEMPs proposed by other services? That is, taking relevance and effectiveness into account, is this a wise investment for DoD as a whole? Analyses at this higher level of trade-space are quite daunting and challenging.

From the above, it seems evident that the most valuable contributions of the Independent Evaluators will be at the last two levels and, perhaps, more specifically at the last level—where the trade-space is in terms of comparing the return on investment among all types of operational capabilities by all of the services. To determine the best marginal return on investment, all players—force elements and their associated CONEMPs—must compete against a common measure of outcome that can be meaningfully quantified and calculated. That is, analysts must be able to establish, quantitatively, the relationship between incremental investments in a particular concept and marginal increases in one or more common metrics.

As the trade-space expands, the common metric, by necessity, becomes more encompassing and more difficult to calculate or even estimate. However, simply grasping the idea that the name of the game is best marginal return among various investments is an important step forward. At least our horizon of thought and scope will be expanded. Thus, the Independent Evaluators should have their primary focus on identifying the best marginal return among all types of operational capabilities. This is quite distinct from a focus on determining the most cost-effective manner of accomplishing a stated task.

The Independent Evaluators, then, serve as honest brokers among the Proponents, each of whom can be expected to be promoting concepts intended to enhance operational capabilities relevant to his or her set of challenges. The work of the Independent Evaluators should help the Secretary and the Chief of Staff to understand and to compare the value of these concepts. It should also be directly relevant to advocating those concepts deemed worthy of taking forward to the Top-Level Deciders.

There is probably an optimum level at which to engage in quantitative analyses intended to inform decisions about investments to modernize capabilities. We submit that this optimum is at the operational level, as distinct from the task level (which lies one level below) and as distinct from the campaign level (which is one level above). The objective of these analyses is to define the best CONEMP for achieving improved capabilities within a stated operational objective.

This is not to say that we need not address matters at the campaign level; certainly we need to know about the relevance of various types of operational capabilities. However, assessments at the campaign level are not generally a matter of number crunching. Rather, insights regarding the contributions of a particular concept and its associated systems must derive from sound military judgment. If, in scenario after scenario, certain types of forces (and their attendant CONEMPs) are not involved, then the question of relevance arises:

Is this particular type of force (or the operational capabilities this type of force provides) really relevant?

The above is not intended to discourage attempts at quantifying the trades among investments in various concepts at the campaign level. Analysts should assess trades quantitatively at as high a level as is appropriate, and they make no apology about establishing "relevance" at the higher levels according to a well-tested approach called military judgment. To this end, the Independent Evaluators could include a group of retired senior officers.

The Secretary and the Chief of Staff should task the Independent Evaluators to provide what analysis they can muster to assist in the advocacy of preferred CONEMPs to the Top-Level Deciders.

The Secretary and the Chief of Staff must make the case that resources should be allocated to implement the preferred CONEMP for improving the capability to achieve one or more operational objectives. The Proponents may be called upon to make their case in two distinct ways: First, if there exists a broad consensus within DoD that a certain operational capability should be improved, the Proponents will focus on arguments that this is the best CONEMP for achieving this particular type of operational capability. These arguments are quite relevant when there are different CONEMPs still in contention to achieve a stated type of operational capability. However, in many cases the argument is not about competing CONEMPs to achieve a stated type of operational capability, but rather about the relevance of that particular type of operational capability in the first place. In these cases, proponents must be prepared to show why resources should be allocated to enhancing the operational capability addressed by their CONEMP.

In any event, it behooves the Proponents to have a clear understanding on which type of argument they face. The Proponents could easily win the first argument (this is indeed the best CONEMP for achieving this particular operational capability) and lose the second argument (even so, there are better marginal returns if resources are allocated to implement another CONEMP for achieving a quite different operational objective).

Chapter Seven

ORGANIZATIONAL MATTERS

We have presented a model for modernizing the operational capabilities of the Air Force. A one-for-one relationship between this model and the organizational charts and structure of the Air Force is not obvious.

THE DEFINER

The Definer should reside within the Air Staff. Ideally, the Definer would report to a lieutenant general charged solely with modernizing.

THE PROPONENTS

There could be seven Proponents (teams)—each headed by a brigadier general. They would report to the deputy chief of staff (DCS) for modernization. The teams could be organized as follows:

Team One: Gain Freedom to Operate

- Establish access

- Gain air superiority

- Gain space superiority

Team Two: Provide Control of the Operation of Forces

Team Three: Provide Strategic Air Mobility

Team Four: Fight and Attain Desired Effects in Conflicts

Team Five: Protect the Homeland

Team Six: Conduct Global Strikes

Team Seven: Conduct Other Operations

- Maintain global awareness

- Provide a stabilizing presence in key regions

- Provide humanitarian assistance

Directing the Definers and the Proponents and all they do would be the sole responsibility of the DCS for modernization. More than any other single officer, this person would be responsible for setting the direction of the Air Force of the future.[1]

THE CONCEIVERS-AT-LARGE

The Conceivers-at-Large can be almost anywhere:

- In the technology part of AFMC, but in an organization specifically recognized and chartered for the purpose of defining concepts to accomplish military tasks. This function is different from the charter of maturing technologies and reviewing the state-of-art of various technologies.

- Within Air Combat Command, Air Force Space Command, Air Mobility Command, and Air Force Special Operations Command.

- The Air Force Scientific Advisory Board (SAB) could be a fertile field for defining new CONEXs. It should be tasked (and challenged) explicitly to do so. Otherwise, this body will tend to focus on reviews of the performance levels of various technologies.

- RAND's Project AIR FORCE could establish a group of Conceivers dedicated to providing grist for the mill for the Proponents. This

_____

[1]Indeed, the DCS for modernization could be given the title of the "transformer" of the Air Force.

group, heavily populated by technologists, would serve all seven teams.

- Contractors, as well, represent a fertile source of new CONEXs.

THE INDEPENDENT EVALUATORS

One group of Independent Evaluators should reside in the Air Force Studies and Analysis Agency. They would devote their energies and talents to the daunting analyses set forth earlier in this report, divesting themselves of lesser endeavors.

THE PROVIDERS

The Providers reside in the major commands: Air Combat Command, Air Mobility Command, Air Force Space Command, Air Force Special Operations Command, and the Air Force Materiel Command. As noted above, the Air Force's major operating commands participate actively in the formation of new CONEXs relevant to their operations. However, their primary responsibility is to implement new concepts as directed. When the Providers are allocated resources to implement a proposed concept, generally their commands proceed to do so in a professional manner and produce the desired output—relevant and powerful operational capabilities for the combatant commanders.

Chapter Eight

REMARKS ABOUT DOCUMENTS

There now exists a bewildering array of documents and procedures attendant to the process of modernizing. They include Mission Area Analyses (MAA), Mission Need Analyses (MNA), Mission Need Statements (MNS), Operational Requirements Documents (ORD), Analyses of Multiple Concepts or Analyses of Alternatives (AoA), and others. Should the general framework as set forth herein be adopted by all services, the analyses, and the documents on these analyses, could be dramatically clarified and the entire modernizing process could be streamlined.

The logic is straightforward. The model for modernizing proposed in this report is clear about the key decisions to be made and what actor makes them. The key decisions are:

- The service Secretary and the Chief of Staff decide what challenges (missions, operational objectives) the service intends to strive to meet or fulfill.

   — War games examining a range of scenarios could help inform these decisions.

- The Proponents explore new concepts to meet these challenges and from time to time propose to the Secretary and the Chief that they implement a particular concept.

   — An AoA helps inform these decisions.

- The Secretary and the Chief then decide which concepts they will propose to the Top-Level Deciders.

   — The same AoA helps to inform this decision.

- The Top-Level Deciders determine whether to implement the concept as proposed by the service.

    — They require certain analyses by PA&E and others to inform this decision.

    — The AoA prepared earlier will be useful here.

- Once the decision is made to implement a particular concept, documents attendant to the process of acquiring any system defined in the concept record *what* is being acquired and *how* (as distinct from *whether* to implement the concept in the first place).

One can see from the above that once we know the actors, what they do, and what they decide, the analyses and documents required to inform and record these decisions are greatly clarified and the analyses become far more purposeful and less numerous. Specifically, there is a test for any analysis or document: What decision by which actor does this analysis inform? If the answer is not readily apparent and logical, then there should be no requirement for the analysis or the document.

The operative word above is "requirement." The services are at liberty to conduct any analysis they see fit. The point is that the CJCS or the Secretary of Defense should direct only those analyses and documents that meet the test suggested above.

BIBLIOGRAPHY

Birkler, J. L., C. R. Neu, and Glenn A. Kent, *Gaining New Military Capability: An Experiment in Concept Development*, RAND, MR-912-OSD, 1998.

Department of Defense Directive No. 5000.1, *The Defense Acquisition System*, USD(AT&L), October 23, 2000.

Deputy Secretary of Defense memorandum, *Defense Acquisition*, Attachment 2, p. 4, October 30, 2002. (See http://dod5000. dau.mil.)

Kent, Glenn A., and David E. Thaler, *A New Concept for Streamlining Up-Front Planning*, RAND, MR-271-AF, 1993.

Thaler, David E., *Strategies to Tasks: A Framework for Linking Means and Ends*, RAND, MR-300-AF, 1993.

U.S. Code, Title 10, Sec. 8013.